I'm N Sixty

Male Edition

Jake Adie

jadie
BOOKS

First Published by Jadie Books Ltd 2005
Revised edition 2008
Reprinted 2009

ISBN 0 9549354 1 1

Illustrations by Ian West

Typesetting by Jake Adie

Printed & bound by
York Publishing Services Ltd
64 Hallfield Road
Layerthorpe
York
YO317ZQ

For the not so old,
not so middle-aged,
not so sure

Other Not Really Titles

I'm Not Really 18 (female edition)
I'm Not Really 18 (male edition)
I'm Not Really 30 (female edition)
I'm Not Really 30 (male edition)
I'm Not Really 40 (female edition)
I'm Not Really 40 (male edition)
I'm Not Really 50 (female edition)
I'm Not Really 50 (male edition)
I'm Not Really 60 (female edition)
I'm Not Really 70 (female edition)
I'm Not Really 70 (male edition)
I'm Not Really Pregnant
I'm Not Really Getting Married (female edition)
I'm Not Really Getting Married (male edition)
I'm Not Really Moving House
I'm Not Really Retiring
I'm Not Really a Grandmother
I'm Not Really a Grandfather
I've Not Really Passed My Test
I'm Not Really a Cricketer
I'm Not Really a Footballer
I'm Not Really a Rugby Player
I'm Not Really a Golfer
It's Not Really Christmas

Me Sixty?

This is going to be difficult. Don't quite know where to start. You're going to have to concentrate on this. You see, very soon, I'm not going to be sixty. Yes, that's right, not. Not sixty. Trouble is, I don't know what I *am* going to be. Just know it won't be sixty. Can't be. All right, I will have had a similar amount of birthdays to normal sixty-year-olds — okay, if you want to be pedantic, the same amount. *Exactly* the same. That better? But it makes no difference. What I'm trying to say is I still won't be sixty. Really, it was only a few years ago that I was in my mid-forties. No more than four or five I'm sure. Maybe seven. But not enough for me to be sixty.

You see, I'm nothing like an SYO. Different in every respect. D'you think I don't know an SYO when I see one? They're distinctly different to younger people like me. People who've been around a bit. Mixed with all sorts. Been everywhere. SYOs don't do those things. Do they? Course they don't. They just, well, they sort of, er, kind of spend most of their time being, well, old. That's it, old. Not ancient, I'll grant you, just old. Well, they're not middle-aged, are they? That's forties, fifties. No, they're a different generation. The older generation. You know that, don't you? They've been

around for years.
All look the
same. Same
clothes, same
miserable faces,
same pot-bellies.
Identical. In fact,
I wouldn't be at
all surprised if
many of them
were well into
their seventies or
eighties these
days. They have
different names
as well. Alf, Bert,
Arthur, Fred.
Can't be sixty if
you don't have a
name like that.
Mine's not even

similar. And they speak differently. Know-it-all sort of talk. And give the impression they have better taste. In music for instance. And food. Yes, food. They know why their food is better. Never tried yours but still know. Clever, eh? Never tried it but know all about it. Huh! Well I'm not like that. I would never criticize

I'm Not Really Sixty

10

other folks' opinions just for the sake of it. No point. Not polite. Nothing to *do* with me. Unless, of course, they try to defend those stupid, repetitive, pop songs they listen to. That's different. You have to draw a line somewhere. Or those disgusting foreign dishes they eat nowadays. Nothing wrong with attempting to educate the young. Spending good money on that oriental muck. You wouldn't get me inside one of *those* restaurants. But that's nothing to do with sixty. That's just common sense, experience. No, what I'm talking about is prejudice. Condemning without reason. Being plain awkward for no purpose other than it's what SYOs are supposed to do. I wouldn't behave like that. Wouldn't dream of it. You've only to look at the way real SYOs choose their . . .

That's if they do choose them. Let's be honest, they look more as though they were given away. So far out of date it would be hard to imagine *anyone* paying for them. Although, thinking about it, I'm having trouble picturing what sort of shop would stock them. I know where I buy *my* clothes and you certainly don't

Clothes

get them there. But then, of course, I'm that much younger. Still wearing denims. Not those tight ones or those big, outsize, baggy ones. No, the in-between, comfortable, trendy ones. Perhaps they don't buy them any more. Maybe they bought heavy duty clothes when they were in fashion and they just sort of lasted. Reasonable? I don't know. It might be the case for some of them but there'll always be those who didn't and they'd end up walking around in tatters. No, there must be another answer. How about their partners make them? No, some may not have partners. Well, there must be a shop somewhere that specializes in SYO styles. In some ways they're not that dissimilar to our gear. Take casual zip-up jackets for example. The rest of society wears a variety of designs in all sorts of fabrics so that they can enjoy at least a sense of individuality, don't they? And in all colours too. Some have big pocket flaps and contrasting, brightly-coloured lining. Big zips. Buttons. Big zips *and* buttons. Hoods. No hoods but big, stand-up collars. Cotton. Nylon. Half cotton, half nylon. *Waxed* cotton. Keep you dry in a tropical storm they would. There's no limit is there? We can all look good, we can all keep dry and we can all look different. We can pop into the corner shop on the way home, pick up a loaf of bread, two pints of milk and a regular pack of corn flakes, undo a couple of zips, shove them in and nobody would ever know we'd been shopping.

So why do our dear old SYOs insist on bucking the trend and wearing those boring, plain, nylon, zip-up tops without any of the features that make the rest of us look the business? You know the ones: almost green with matching elasticated, woolly waist- neck- and cuff-bands. And no pockets! What's the use of no pockets? It hardly saves any material. And no shape. One size top to bottom. Well, I don't own one of those. Wouldn't have a clue where to buy one. And besides, it would never fit over the top of my brown, Harris tweed, sports jacket. There's no doubt about it, SYOs live in a different world. Different for the sake of it. How else could you account for their . . .

Music

Music's personal, isn't it? Everyone to their own and all that. I have no intention of sounding off here about some universal absolute regarding what constitutes good music. It's up to the person concerned. Purely subjective. Whatever moves you, yeah? What causes *me* to press the play button is my

choice and mine alone. And if your idea of harmonic bliss is something I wouldn't wish upon the ears of my worst enemy then that's fine by me. Doesn't matter a jot. I'd rather you didn't insist on my attending a musical appreciation evening at your house but I will defend, to the very end, your right to differ. It

is these
differences that
grant us
individuality.
Our own
distinctive
quality. A label,
if you like.
Something for
which we will be
recognized. Our
very own
personal, unique
and endearing
characteristic.
We don't have to
follow the crowd,
do we. We can do
our own thing.
But if crowds are
our own thing,

then we follow them, right? Doesn't matter. Up to us. No one else. Just you and me. And SYOs, bless them, have a wonderfully wide diversity of musical tastes. May not be yours or mine but they're still able to gain hours of pleasure from them.

Brass bands, that's SYO music. Marches. They're okay.

Don't buy them myself but, no big deal — do some good stuff they do. Bing Crosby, Count Basie, George Formby, Paul Robson, Al Jolson, the Black and White Minstrels, remember them? Max Bygraves. All different but with one important thing in common: all good, wholesome SYO music. They know precisely what they like, what brings the memories of adolescence flooding back in less time than you can utter 'Vera Lynn'. It's the music of their time. The music that holds the key to *their* private moments. Penetrates deep into their emotions. That's what music does to all of us. Finds its way right to the centre of our hearts, stirs up the corpuscles until they start pumping the old ticker like a good'un. Transports us to another land. That's the power of music. Knows no boundaries. Takes us wherever we want to go. My music. Your music. SYO's music. It all does it. Agree? WELL THEN, WHY DON'T THE BLOODY SYOS

APPRECIATE THE FACT LIKE THE REST OF US AND SHUT UP SLAGGING OFF OURS AND EVERYONE ELSE'S MUSIC? There, I've got *that* off my chest. You can see it's been bothering me. Silly really. Just a niggling little irritation. But I apologize for shouting. Just sort of came out. Sorry. Mustn't let them get me down.

Their problem, not mine. I'm completely sorted. Know exactly what I like and I'm jolly well going to go and listen to all my favourite Elvis tracks right now. That's right, Elvis. Elvis Presley. And if there are any SYOs listening, too bad. You probably won't have even heard of him. Strictly for the youngsters.

Always has been. Good, reliable, solid rock 'n' roll. That's what I call real music. Oops! Do you think I've upset them? Eh? Hope not. Probably have. Probably all gone off for a sulk. Reckon? Well, let's keep our voices down a bit and take advantage of their temporary absence. How about a giggle at their attitude towards . . .

Sex

This will have to remain one of life's great mysteries. The paradox to beat all paradoxes. The mother of all imponderables. The one question, which no matter how hard we try, we're just going to have to accept will never be answered. A problem, I know but there you are. Don't waste your time, you'll never get to the

bottom of it. It goes like this: how come SYOs had children? Seems impossible, I know, but there is irrefutable evidence to suggest they did. We *know* they did but we don't know *how* they did. Remarkable, or what? A bit like the virgin birth I suppose. Although that was purported to have taken place a couple of millennia ago and, without wanting to sound disrespectful or unduly controversial, we have to realise that a good few gallons have passed under the bridges of history in the intervening years which must cast some doubt on the tale's accuracy. Just a smidgen surely. But here, now, at the dawning of the twenty-first century we are unable to cite apocrypha as being responsible for our predicament. We know it's happened.

So, to put it as succinctly as I can: how on earth did a whole generation come into being when their alleged mums and dads didn't like sex? I mean, it is a fairly integral part of the whole process, isn't it? It's too late now to find out for sure but it is rather puzzling, don't you think? All the evidence would suggest that their aversion knew few bounds. The mere mention of the subject on TV has them fumbling for the remote control let alone an actual picture of a pair of boobs or a willy. "Disgusting, shouldn't be allowed", you can just hear them, can't you? Recoil at the thought of anything remotely connected with the matter. Well, I'd like to hear them tell that to God. He wouldn't be too happy. All the trouble he went to to see that we actually *wanted* to reproduce and they think it's disgusting. I thank the Lord

I'll never be sixty. Couldn't entertain the prospect of being repelled by all that lovely flesh. And then they come out with this ridiculous story about not being allowed to do it before you're married. What is that all about? What, I ask you, did God think he was doing when he programmed puberty to kick in two years before we were due to sit our 'O' level mocks? Was it *his* idea that we should somehow suppress the urge right the way through our course work, into the sixth form, two more years studying for 'A' levels, three years at uni, year out travelling, job searching, career development, courting, sudden change of partner, more courting, getting engaged, saving like hell, short period of uncertainty, set date, more uncertainty, cancel date, change mind again, set another date, book church, invite guests, take vows, smile for the cameras, eat, mess up speech, get drunk, change into going away outfit, say

goodbye to
guests, go away,
taxi, hotel, check
in, room key,
suitcases, climb
stairs, unlock
door, carry
partner across
threshold,
bathroom,
undress, bed?
Bloody hell,
you'd forget what
you were
supposed to do in
the first place. I
mean, it was a
long time ago.
No, no, no. God
may move in
mysterious ways,

I won't dispute that, but he wouldn't cock the whole thing up from start to finish. Make a monumental balls-up of the whole business. There's got to be another explanation. Got to be. I've got *my* theory. Only a theory, mind you. Think there's a fair chance that aliens had something to do with it. Well,

they could have.
Must be an
answer
somewhere.
Anyway, as I
said, I stand
absolutely no
chance of
becoming a real
SYO with my
tendencies. Not
likely. If SYOs
spent all those
years in
abstinence you
can take it from
me that they
never had the
urge in the first
place. Couldn't
have done.

SYOs are just
different. Look at
the way they
choose their . . .

Cars

I'm serious. Look at the cars they drive around in. Normal non-SYOs wouldn't be seen dead in them. They act as if the things are just for going from A to B. Absurd. Mind you, if you had to travel about in one of those, you'd only *want* to go from A to B. Certainly wouldn't want to stop off on the way. Or go racing off to C.

Or pull into the pub car park or cruise along the seafront. Not likely. Make a laughing stock of yourself. Never be able to show your face again. No, if going from A to B is all you've got to do then I won't argue. Maybe they have a point. But there is such a thing as self-respect. Dignity. Can't have much of that if you insist on ferrying yourself around in a Morris 1100. Or an Austin Cambridge. They just weren't designed with street cred in mind, were they? But then what's the point in trying to make an impression if you're an SYO anyway? Non-SYOs like me, perhaps. Fellas with age immunity. Nothing to worry about at all.

Drive whatever you like. No problem.
But you know why they opt for those dreadful machines in the first place, eh? What makes them actually spend money on them? Ehm? It's because they go with the zip-up tops. The almost-green ones. Sort of blend. Don't you think? Can't argue with that. They do somehow look

right together. Armani suits and Morris Minors don't quite strike the right note. Just a touch incongruous wouldn't you say? Although, come to think of it, there is a strong tendency these days for all sorts of obsolete vehicles to be re-categorized into the 'Classic Car' genre. Anything seems to qualify providing it's been patched up with filler, painted over and polished up a bit. And they seem to be earning themselves all manner of accolades for no other reason than their age. And I must admit that a trendy outfit could, in some circumstances, look rather cool against the backdrop of a 'sixty-four Healey or even a 'fifty-nine

Zepher. Ehm, would look kinda smart. Hadn't quite seen it like that before. Perhaps those old SYO motors aren't so uncool after all. Not so un-cred as you might think. Wouldn't attract so much attention at those Classic Car shows they hold nowadays. Places get crowded. Positively swarming with all types. Ehm,

maybe I was wrong about their cars. Misjudged them somewhat. Wasn't really thinking straight. Picture certainly looks a little different if you give it some thought.
But hold on. There's something a bit odd about this. Can't quite put my finger on it but something doesn't feel quite right. SYO cars

aren't so bad after all but SYOs, well they don't somehow fit in. What is it? Seems a bit peculiar. Cool motors, SYOs? Ah, I've got it. Of course. Am I some sort of idiot or what? It's obvious. What a complete twerp. SYOs' cars *are* cool. Probably always have been. But not with SYOs in them. Get it? They've had to wait all these years for young people to make them look good. Nothing wrong with the motors — just the SYOs. All seems clear now don't you think? Glad I don't have these problems with my Austin Allegro. Little beauty that is. Bought it new. Be a classic itself one day. Another perfect example of my non-SYO status.

Cars

Not that you need any more convincing, but, I must mention a subject that always tickles me; have you ever noticed their attitude towards . . .

Bit of a contradiction of terms that. SYOs, work? Doesn't have quite the same rapport as port and lemon. Or Morcambe and Wise. Don't really have a lot to do with each other. I know they turn up on time every day. And don't generally pack away until it's time to go. But as for productivity, well

what can you say? I mean, what can you say without offending them? Well, nothing. Nothing at all. And that's not down to me. Not some quirky attitude on my part. *I* haven't got any reason to have it in for them. Just reporting things as they are. The truth. The truth about what our SYO friends get up to while they

should be working.
I'm sure they don't *mean* to be a burden. Probably think they're pulling as hard as the next man. But us youngsters know the difference, don't we. It's not their fault that they don't have a clue about modern technology. In their days they were taught properly, weren't they? Listened to

their teachers, their bosses and believed every word they said. "This is how it's done lad. Now you make sure you do exactly as you're told or you'll have me to answer to." Yeah? Heard that somewhere before? Course you have. And that's precisely what they did. For fifty-odd years. They believed every word of it. That's how it should be done. Never thought to question it. Just got on with it year in, year out. Amazing. If teacher said, *"Add the units up first then carry the tens over to the next column and add them in with the tens. Then do the same with the hundreds and so on and so forth"*, then that's what they did. Forever. And if the boss told 'em to keep the dockets all safe 'n tidy in a bulldog clip hanging from a drawing pin attached to the back of the office door, then that's also what they did. They believed every word. And over the ensuing years the words took on a sort of carved-in-stone status. Never to be spoken in vain. The methods became sacrosanct. Beyond criticism. Immune from the need for future revision. Well, it might have seemed all okay at the time but things have changed over the years. Just a bit! The rule book has been rewritten. And not just once. We run the whole show differently today. Everyone can see that. Doesn't take a genius. Things move faster now. More mouths to feed. The population's grown out of all proportion and we can't afford to sit around on our backsides doing long multiplication and adopting clerical methods that date back to the dark ages. IT'S THE SECOND MILLENNIUM FOR GOD'S SAKE.

MODERN
TECHNOLOGY
IS HERE TO
HELP US NOT
HINDER US.
WAKE UP
PLEASE.
Look, I've said
enough on this
subject, made my
point and can't
waste any more
time. Not that I
haven't got any
more time.
Plenty of it.
Absolutely
oodles. But then
I'm no SYO. Not
hampered with
their outmoded,

inefficient, obsolete ways of doing things. Give me a slide rule and half-a-dozen lever-arch files any day — you won't catch me messing around with old technology when there's work to be done. Bit baffling, this subject, don't you think? I mean, I've obviously convinced you by now that I'll never qualify as an SYO but you're probably wondering what it is I'll actually be. Age-wise, what will I be called? Difficult, eh? Well, I'm no wiser than you. Got no idea. Just avoid the topic whenever it arises. No choice. If there was just one shred of doubt it may be different. But there isn't. I mean, they don't even eat the same . . .

I'm Not Really Sixty

Food

They eat SYO food. Doesn't even look like ours. Cooked differently, has different ingredients. Bears little resemblance, in fact, to proper food. Even smells different. Nothing like the healthy wholesome items I pick up at the supermarket. Different shelves. They must have a separate section

especially for SYOs.
Somewhere round the back. Never seen it myself but then I only ever need to shop where the young people shop.
And it's cheaper being modern like me. Must be — economies of scale principle. If more people buy it, it has to be less expensive to make. Adam Smith, division of labour and all

that stuff. Don't really understand it but if they teach it in universities it must be right. So, not only do you benefit by the superior taste of modern food, it's far more economical as well. Being a non-SYO pays all sorts of dividends. And that's without even considering the ghastly taste of the stuff they consume. Meat puddings, tripe and onions, liver and bacon, semolina, tapioca, luncheon meat, spam, processed peas. Need I go on? I've probably put you off your lunch by now anyway. Sorry. Why do they eat all that muck? I mean, what's the point of wrapping lovely, delicious, nutritious pieces of best beef in a thick, stodgy coat of suet? It's disgusting. All the goodness from the meat, all the rich, succulent juices, just get soaked up into the horrible goo surrounding it. Then cause you to perform some gross exercise involving the tongue and forefinger when the whole sodden mass ends up stuck to the roof of your mouth. Nasty habit.

Although, I suppose there could be a method to their madness. Come to think of it, wasn't the whole point of hiding the meat in the first place simply a ploy to disguise the fact that what's been put inside should really have been given to the dog? Or better, the bin? Wasn't that the original theory behind the whole sordid practice? Okay, maybe there was a need once upon a time to conserve rations. To stretch them as far into the ensuing week as was physically possible. Yeah, all right, times weren't always as good, I know. And I don't mean to be disrespectful to those who had no choice in the matter. If meat pudding was the only answer then meat pudding it should jolly well have been. We're not going to fall out over that. But really, these days? These second millennium days when the weekly provisions cost a mere fraction of what they did all those years ago? There was a time when all that was left of Pop's wages, after a couple of Friday evening pints, barely met the

Saturday morning shop at the corner store. Things were different then. But we now live in the age of SDI (surplus disposable income) and I'm afraid there is no longer any excuse. You can keep your meat pud if you like but, if it makes no difference to you, I'll stick with my healthy, nutritious, full-of-natural-goodness beefburgers thank you very much.

Mind you, if you are a meat-pud-inclined SYO there can't be many opportunities to grab yourself a quick meal these days. Just imagine pulling up at the drive-thru, winding down the window and yelling out, "Two regular McPuds, one large boiled carrots and onions and two jam turnovers". They'd call for the men in white coats. So where do these strange individuals manage to eat when they go on their . . .

Holidays

I suppose we'll just have to use our imagination. But, more to the point, where do they go on their hols? Have you ever seen them? Can't say I have. Benidorm? San Antonio? Rhodes? St. Tropez? No, don't remember seeing any of them there. Funny. Must go somewhere. They certainly take time off work don't they? So,

what do they do with their time? Majorca? No. The Algarve? No. Well, I think I've seen foreign SYOs in most of these places but that's different. We're talking about British ones. Never seen them there. So, where do they go? Are there any other places? I've never really thought about it before. Let me concentrate —

just amuse
yourselves for a
moment while I
get my brain into
gear. Right,
Caner . . . Carrib
. . . Malag . . .
Cypr . . . Tusc . . .
Malt . . . ehm . . .
ehm . . . Flo.
GOT IT!
FLORIDA!
Sorry, didn't
mean to shout.
Florida? Well,
possibly. No,
perhaps not.
Can't remember
seeing any of
them over there.
Oh well, I give

up. Any suggestions? Anyone else want to have a go? Eh? What? Say that again. What's that? Ehm? No, he's a boxer, isn't he? Sorry?
'Bognor.'
Bognor?
'B-O-G-N-O-R?'
Where on earth is that? I've never heard of it.
'On the south coast.'
Is it? Where abouts?
'Sussex.'

Sussex? Well it's a new one on me. What's it like then? What do you mean it's difficult to explain? Try, go on tell us what's there. Tell us what's so special about this place Bognor that causes SYOs not to bother going to ordinary holiday destinations. Tell us why they go. Come on.

'Pebbly beach, white, stucco

guest houses . . .'
Yeah, go on.
'Big waves, cold winds . . .'
Really? Any more?
'Beach huts, deck-chairs, cafes . . .'
Is that it? Nothing else? No? Are you sure? Are you absolutely sure there's nothing else at this Bognor place in Sussex?
'Sorry, I Can't think of anything.'

Well why do they go there? What do they do there? *They sit on the beach wearing thick, woolly jumpers and read newspapers.'* You're kidding me. You're having me on. They really do that? Why? What for? And how do you get there? Drive? *'You can but they don't.'* This is getting complicated.

What do you mean, *'You can drive there but they don't'*? How on earth do they get there, walk, hop, crawl, swim?
'They go by coach with hundreds of other SYOs.'
Now you're taking the mickey. Are you telling me that they all get together and travel in great big buses? All the way down to Bognor? You are?

That means they must all go at the same time. What happens in Bognor after they all go home? *'They don't always go home, they often stay down there to live.'* They *live* in Bognor? No, please, I think we'd better leave it there. My head's beginning to hurt. Probably some government run organization I reckon. Compulsory for all SYOs. Thank God I'm going to dodge that one. Must make a note to avoid the place. Might never get out alive. Like entering a black hole. But surely, they can't just sit on the pebbly, cold, windy beach all day, they must spend some of their time pursuing their . . .

It is often said
that a true
indication of a
man's character
will be found by
studying his
hobbies: his
pastimes, his
sporting
interests. These
will provide an
accurate
measure of how
he feels he
should slot into
society. His
vocational role, if
you like. And it
is in this area
where, although
I say it myself, I

Hobbies

can be most positively identified as deserving of lifelong membership to the non-SYO club. But our SYO friend, as you will see, is not quite so fortunate. Being, understandably, devoid of any effective means of executing his own ideas in this regard, he is automatically allowed access to the underside of society's altruistic wings and allocated an official, albeit non-negotiable, pastime. He, of course, doesn't see it this way and it is just as well. He truly believes that he *wants* to play bowls. Wants to sign up with the local club and wear a waistcoat on Tuesday and Thursday afternoons. But that's fine. So long as he thinks it's *his* choice there's no harm done, is there? The system has worked for years and has proved its worth many times over. No one has ever been known to have seen through it although it is possible that sheer embarrassment could have caused those more perceptive individuals amongst us to keep any such thoughts to themselves. After all, there'd be no obvious personal gain in blowing the gaff so to speak. Might as well toe the line and enjoy it. What better option is there? But the pure ingenuity of the process where the state, in a sense, manages to coerce each participant into accepting a convincing substitution for his own free-will is nothing short of mind-blowing. And to hinge the whole ethos of the game on a simple, tactile, psychological device whereby each player, in order to become the victor, is encouraged to hurl a token, sacrificial black, devil-inspired, aptly follically-free, cranium form (representing the primordial, masculine aggression instinct to defeat all rival males), at a smaller, passive, white, spherical object portraying the all-forgiving creator, is its ultimate *pièce de résistance*. Who could compete with that? Works every time. *They* are systematically deluded into believing they retain the ability to exercise choice while *we*, the state if you wish, successfully free the supermarket check-out counters of their confusing, encumbering presence twice every week. In short, it lets the rest of us shop in peace. Everyone's happy. Brilliant! What better way to conclude this tome by illustrating the ultimate distinction between yours truly and standard, off-the-peg SYOs than to use this brief cameo of life beyond fifty-nine as it is for the vast majority of our fellow, aging folk? But do your best to keep it from them. Don't want anyone getting upset, do we?